A circuit diagram

It is useful to be able to draw a diagram of how the wires, the batteries and the bulb are connected up. However, not all batteries and light bulbs look the same, so the circuit diagram uses simple symbols instead of pictures (Pictures 2, 3 and 4).

In Picture 5, symbols are used to make a circuit diagram that matches Picture 1.

Notice that the wires in a circuit diagram are always drawn as straight lines with right angle bends. This just makes it easier to follow the path of electricity.

Summary
- A circuit is a loop from a power supply through all of the components and back to the power supply.
- A circuit can be drawn using symbols.
- Symbols are faster to draw and easier to understand than making drawings of the real components.

▲ (Picture 2) This line is the symbol for a wire.

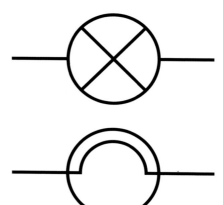

▲ (Picture 3) There are two symbols commonly used for a light bulb. In this book we will use the top one.

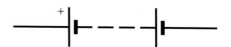

▲ (Picture 4) This is a symbol for two or more batteries connected in a line. All batteries have two connectors, called TERMINALS. The POSITIVE TERMINAL is marked with a + sign.

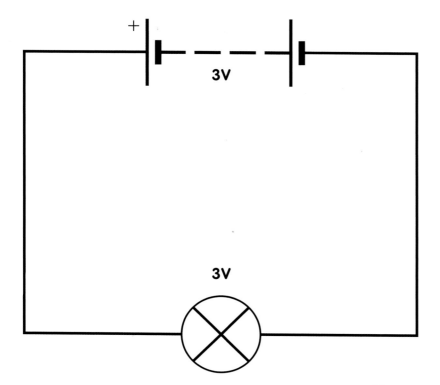

◀ (Picture 5) This is a circuit diagram. It shows each of the components in Picture 1 as symbols.

Weblink: www.CurriculumVisions.com

Switches: breaking the circuit

Switches are used to break the circuit and control the flow of electricity.

A **CURRENT** flows when all of the parts of a circuit make at least one loop from the **NEGATIVE TERMINAL** to the positive terminal of the battery.

The current flows because every part of the circuit is connected. If one part of the circuit is not connected to the next, no current flows and the circuit does not work.

The switch

A **SWITCH** reliably breaks and remakes a circuit.

You can see how a switch works in Pictures 1 and 2. When the switch is turned on (closed), the contacts are pushed together and the bulb lights up; when the switch is off, the contacts spring apart and the bulb goes out.

Notice that, although the contacts move inside the switch and the light goes on and off, the symbols for a switch and a light bulb never change (Picture 3). The symbols show just the parts of the circuit and not what happens in the circuit.

Using combinations of switches

Switches can be used like the points in a train-shunting yard. By clever use of switches, some parts can be disconnected from the circuit, or switched back on again.

▼ **(Picture 1) The switch is at the 'on' position. Notice that the contacts are closed. Notice also that the symbol for the switch on the circuit diagram in Picture 3 does not change. This is because the circuit just shows you how the components are linked up, not what they do.**

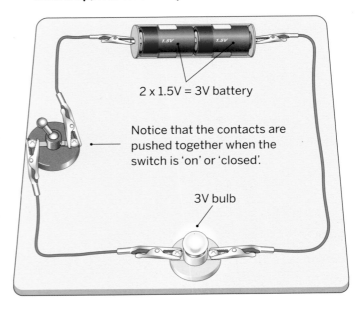

2 x 1.5V = 3V battery

Notice that the contacts are pushed together when the switch is 'on' or 'closed'.

3V bulb

▼ **(Picture 2) The circuit when the switch is off.**

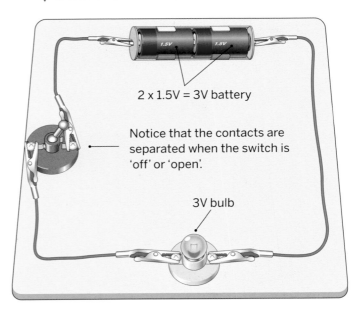

2 x 1.5V = 3V battery

Notice that the contacts are separated when the switch is 'off' or 'open'.

3V bulb

Weblink: www.CurriculumVisions.com

9010194868

Changing circuits

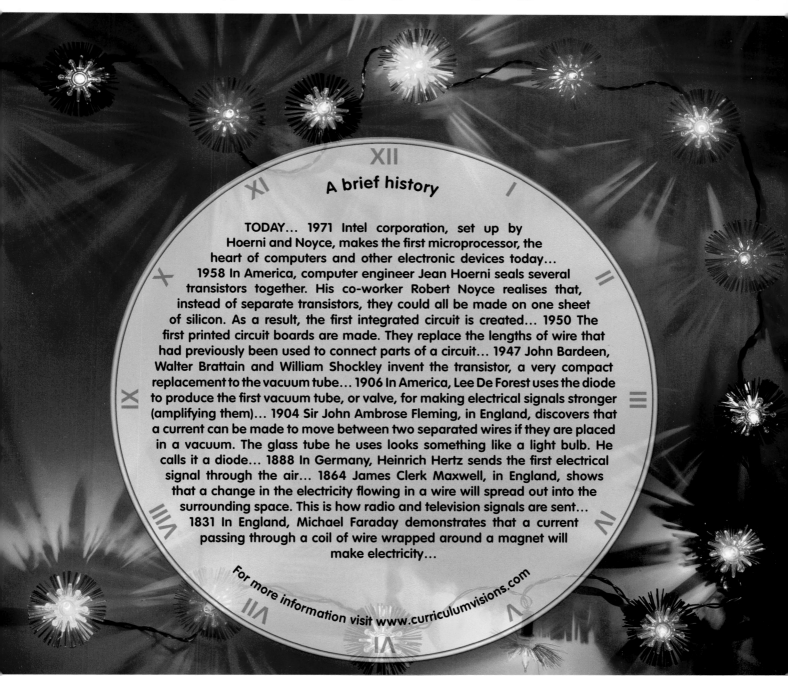

A brief history

TODAY... 1971 Intel corporation, set up by Hoerni and Noyce, makes the first microprocessor, the heart of computers and other electronic devices today... 1958 In America, computer engineer Jean Hoerni seals several transistors together. His co-worker Robert Noyce realises that, instead of separate transistors, they could all be made on one sheet of silicon. As a result, the first integrated circuit is created... 1950 The first printed circuit boards are made. They replace the lengths of wire that had previously been used to connect parts of a circuit... 1947 John Bardeen, Walter Brattain and William Shockley invent the transistor, a very compact replacement to the vacuum tube... 1906 In America, Lee De Forest uses the diode to produce the first vacuum tube, or valve, for making electrical signals stronger (amplifying them)... 1904 Sir John Ambrose Fleming, in England, discovers that a current can be made to move between two separated wires if they are placed in a vacuum. The glass tube he uses looks something like a light bulb. He calls it a diode... 1888 In Germany, Heinrich Hertz sends the first electrical signal through the air... 1864 James Clerk Maxwell, in England, shows that a change in the electricity flowing in a wire will spread out into the surrounding space. This is how radio and television signals are sent... 1831 In England, Michael Faraday demonstrates that a current passing through a coil of wire wrapped around a magnet will make electricity...

For more information visit www.curriculumvisions.com

Dr Brian Knapp

Word list

These are some science words that you should look out for as you go through the book. They are shown using CAPITAL letters.

**CIRCUIT,
ELECTRIC CIRCUIT**
A path that links a source of electricity, such as a battery or mains electricity, to devices that use electricity, such as light bulbs or buzzers.

CIRCUIT DIAGRAM
A simple line drawing that shows the components of a circuit and how they are connected.

CURRENT
The flow of electricity through a circuit. Electric current is measured in units called amps (A).

EARTH WIRE
A wire connected to the metal parts of some appliances, such as cookers and heaters, to give a safe route for electricity to flow if a live wire accidentally touches the metal case.

ELECTRICITY
A form of energy.

ELECTRICITY GRID
A network of cables designed to connect power stations with their customers in offices, homes, schools and factories.

FUSE
A piece of fine wire made of a metal with a low melting point. A fuse is designed to melt if the amount of current flowing in a circuit becomes dangerously large.

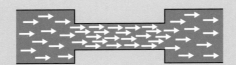

LIVE WIRE
The wire connected to the positive side of the mains electricity supply.

MAINS ELECTRICITY
The electricity supply that is delivered to homes, schools, offices and factories. It is normally 240V.

NEGATIVE TERMINAL
The negative end of a battery.

NEUTRAL WIRE
The mains electricity wire connected to the negative side of the electricity supply.

PARALLEL CIRCUIT
An electrical circuit in which the components are connected side by side (in parallel) to the battery so they all get the same voltage.

POSITIVE TERMINAL
The positive end of a battery.

SERIES CIRCUIT
An electrical circuit in which the battery and all of the other parts are connected end to end in a single loop.

SWITCH
A device for breaking the flow of electricity in a circuit.

TERMINAL
The end of a battery.

VOLTAGE
The electrical 'pressure' that a battery or other source of electricity can provide. It is measured in volts. A single dry battery normally provides 1.5 volts; a mains supply provides 240 volts. Volts can also be written using the symbol 'V'.

Weblink: www.CurriculumVisions.com

Contents

Weblink: www.CurriculumVisions.com

Circuit diagrams

CIRCUIT DIAGRAMS are a way of showing what is happening in a circuit. They are like an electrician's route map.

If we want to use **ELECTRICITY**, we must make a **CIRCUIT**.

To make a circuit, one end of a power supply, such as a battery, must be connected by wires to make a loop that passes through, for example, a light bulb. The loop must end at the *other* end of the power supply.

The simplest kind of circuit connects just two things – for example, a battery and a single light bulb (Picture 1).

▼ **(Picture 1) This is an electrical circuit connecting a battery to a light bulb with two wires. Notice that the combined voltage of the batteries matches the voltage needed by the bulb.**

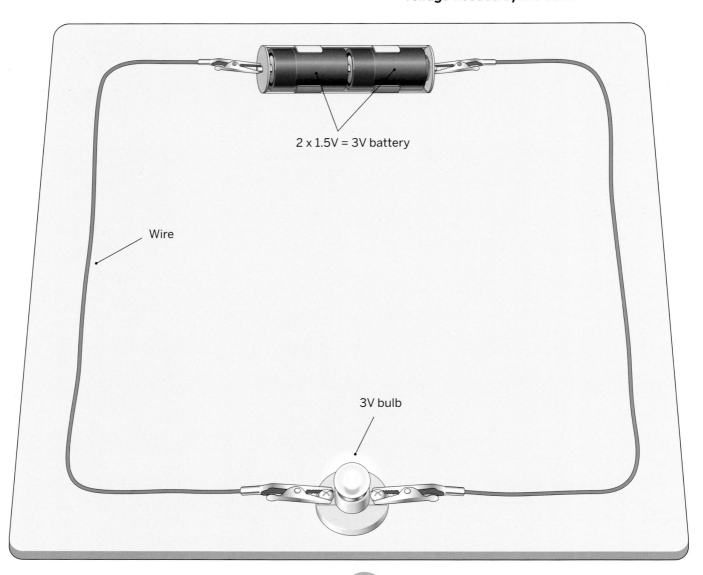

2 x 1.5V = 3V battery

Wire

3V bulb

Picture 4 shows a circuit with two batteries, two switches and two bulbs. Follow it around carefully, starting from the positive (+) terminal of the battery, to see what happens.

Follow the circuit to the left across the top of the circuit. Notice that the wire arrives at a junction – a place where wires are joined together. This is marked **X**.

From this junction there are now two routes for the electricity to follow. Route **A** goes straight down, then through a switch and a bulb.

Route **B** also goes down, to another switch and then to another bulb.

Both routes meet again at a junction at the bottom of the diagram marked **Y**. A single wire leads directly from Y to the negative terminal of the battery. This completes the circuit.

▼ **(Picture 4) Four possible combinations can be achieved with the two switches and two light bulbs in this circuit.**

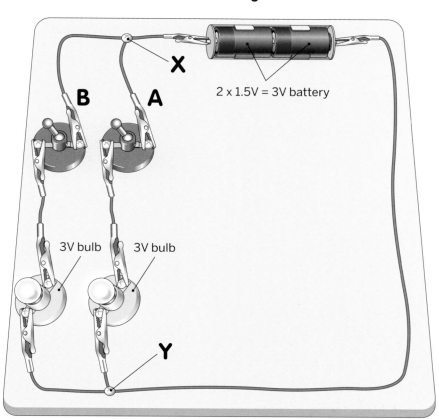

2 x 1.5V = 3V battery

3V bulb   3V bulb

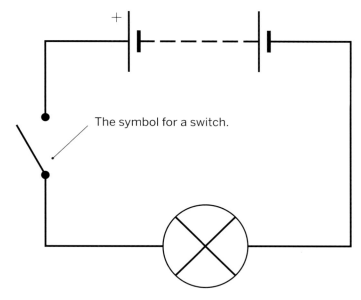

The symbol for a switch.

▲ **(Picture 3) The circuit diagram for the circuit shown in Pictures 1 and 2.**

This is a clever circuit, because we can now have the left-hand bulb switched on while the right-hand bulb is switched off, or the left-hand bulb off and the right-hand bulb on, or both on together, or both off together.

This is the principle on which the lights in your home and school work (see also pages 20 to 21).

Summary
• **Switches control the flow of electricity.**
• **Combinations of switches can give complex control.**

Weblink: www.CurriculumVisions.com

Making bulbs brighter and dimmer

Bulbs get brighter if they have more VOLTAGE, and dimmer if they have to share the voltage with other components.

Picture 1 shows two batteries connected in a loop to a switch and two light bulbs. Picture 2 is a circuit diagram of the same loop. Notice that each of the light bulbs is part of the single loop; *there are no junctions*.

If you were to make this circuit and switch it on, you would find that the bulbs shine more dimly than if the circuit had just one bulb. To make the light bulbs shine more brightly you have to use more batteries.

This shows that when bulbs are connected in a line (in series), the voltages of the batteries and bulbs must always be matched.

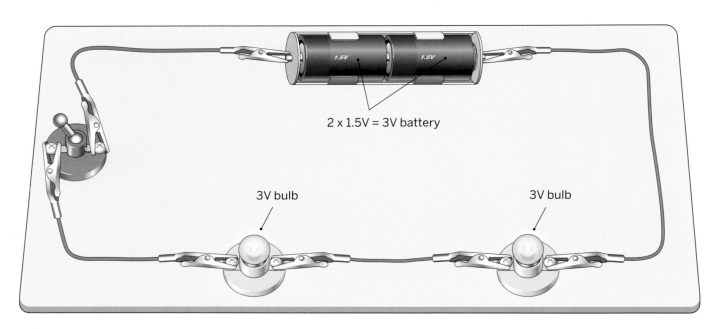

2 x 1.5V = 3V battery

3V bulb

3V bulb

▲ **(Picture 1) This is a SERIES CIRCUIT with two bulbs in a continuous loop.**

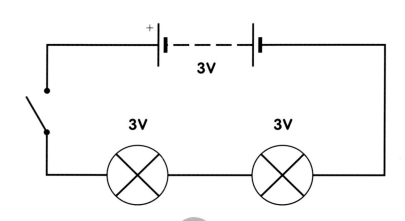

◀ **(Picture 2) The circuit diagram for Picture 1.**

Weblink: www.CurriculumVisions.com

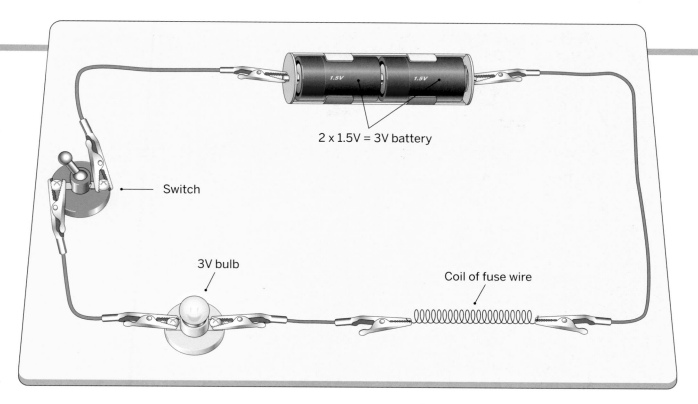

2 x 1.5V = 3V battery

Switch

3V bulb

Coil of fuse wire

The effect of wires

Short, thick wires are very good conductors and use almost no electricity. However, long, fine wires do use up electricity.

Picture 3 shows a coil made of several meters of very fine wire connected in a simple circuit with a bulb, a switch and a battery. The bulb will shine only dimly, showing that the coil of thin wire is using up electricity. We should not be surprised at this, because inside every bulb is a coil of fine wire, called a filament (Picture 4).

Changing the length of the wire

If you connect the coil of wire to the circuit using crocodile clips, you can find out how different lengths of wire affect the brightness of the bulb. You simply connect one of the crocodile clips to various parts of the coil and look at the brightness of the bulb.

▲ (Picture 3) A circuit using a coil of wire such as fuse wire. The loops in the coil should not touch each other.

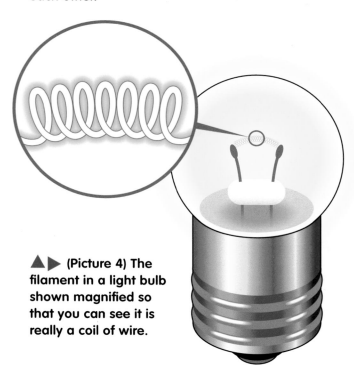

▲▶ (Picture 4) The filament in a light bulb shown magnified so that you can see it is really a coil of wire.

Summary
• **The brightness of a bulb is controlled by the number of components in the circuit. The more bulbs there are, the less voltage there is to make each one work at its best.**

Weblink: www.CurriculumVisions.com

Making motors go faster and slower

A motor can be speeded up and slowed down by changing the voltage it receives.

Just as a light bulb can be made dimmer and brighter by changing the voltage, so the speed of a motor can also be changed.

A modern motor might look complicated, so before we examine how to change its speed, we will first show you how simple a motor really is.

A simple motor

An electric motor uses electricity to make a spindle turn. Picture 1 shows you a version of the first motor ever made. This version is simple enough for you to make.

A copper wire dangles in a metal dish containing salty water. In the centre of the dish is a rod-shaped magnet. When the copper wire and the dish are connected

▼ **(Picture 1) This equipment is a version of the world's first motor, made by Michael Faraday in the 19th century. The salty water allows the wire to move and still keep a circuit.**

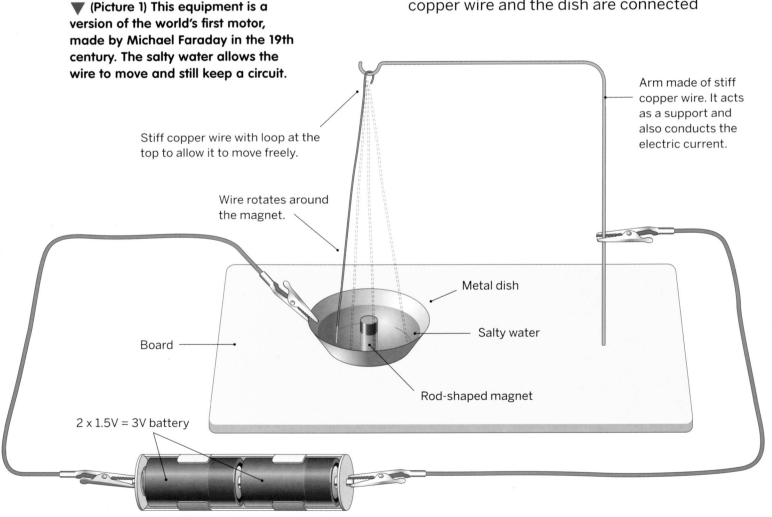

Stiff copper wire with loop at the top to allow it to move freely.

Arm made of stiff copper wire. It acts as a support and also conducts the electric current.

Wire rotates around the magnet.

Metal dish

Salty water

Board

Rod-shaped magnet

2 x 1.5V = 3V battery

to the battery, something astonishing happens. The wire moves away from the magnet and then begins to spin around it.

How the motor works

When the battery is connected, electricity flows through the wire, the salty water (salty water conducts electricity – see pages 14 and 15) and the dish. The electric current flowing through the wire turns it into a magnet. Because the wire is now a magnet, one end of it is pushed away (repelled) by one end of the rod-shaped magnet.

The wire goes around and around the magnet, trying to fall back to rest but, while the current flows, it never can. In this way we have changed electricity into movement. This is the principle of the motor. A modern electric motor (Picture 2) is an 'inside-out' version of the first motor made by Faraday.

Making the motor go faster

The speed of the motor depends on the voltage of the battery, just as the brightness of a bulb depends on the voltage. In the top diagram in Picture 2, the battery gives out 3 volts (3V) because it is made of two 1.5V batteries end to end. The total voltage is found by adding together the voltage of both batteries. If you add another battery (making the total voltage 4.5V), the motor would go faster; if you take one away (leaving just 1.5V) the motor will go slower.

▼ **(Picture 2) A motor turns faster if it is powered by more batteries. However, if too many batteries are used there is a risk of burning out the motor.**

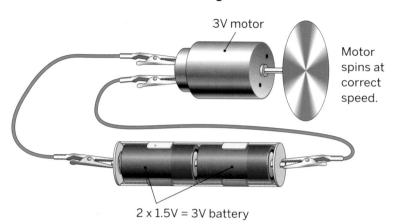

3V motor

Motor spins at correct speed.

2 x 1.5V = 3V battery

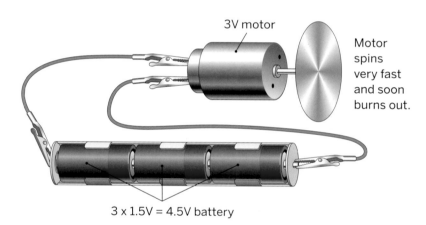

3V motor

Motor spins very fast and soon burns out.

3 x 1.5V = 4.5V battery

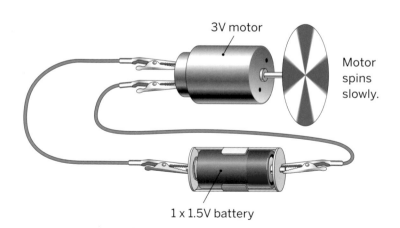

3V motor

Motor spins slowly.

1 x 1.5V battery

Summary
- **The speed at which a motor goes around depends on the voltage sent to the motor; the greater the voltage, the faster the motor turns.**

Weblink: www.CurriculumVisions.com

Parallel circuits

In PARALLEL CIRCUITS, each component has a direct connection to the power supply.

We do not always have to connect components in a line. We can also connect them side by side. When we do this we say the circuit is connected in parallel.

Picture 1 shows three light bulbs connected directly to the same two batteries. This is a simple parallel circuit.

However, you do not have to use as much wire as in Picture 1. Some wires can be shared. Now look at Picture 2, which shows a much neater layout. Here, some wire has been shared. Make sure you see that Pictures 1 and 2 do the same job, and only the layout has changed.

Picture 3 shows the same parallel circuit drawn as a circuit diagram. Notice that, in parallel wiring, wires have to be joined at junctions.

The advantages of parallel wiring

No matter how many components you connect up in parallel, every one will work just as well as when there is only one item connected. Similarly, if one component in a parallel circuit stops working, it will not affect the others. This is because each bulb is directly connected to the battery.

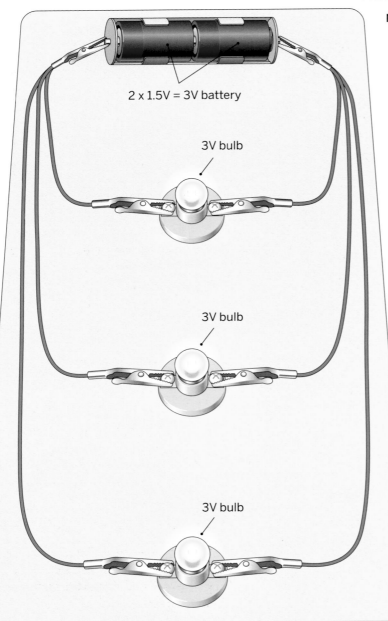

2 x 1.5V = 3V battery

3V bulb

3V bulb

3V bulb

◀ (Picture 1) Three bulbs connected directly to the same battery.

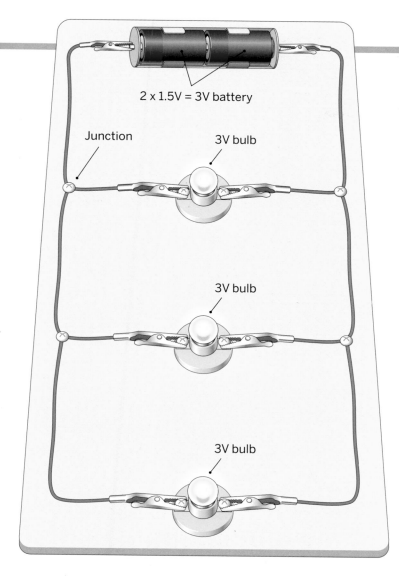

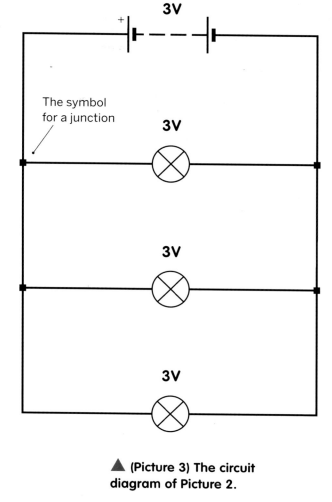

▲ (Picture 3) The circuit diagram of Picture 2.

▲ (Picture 2) Parallel circuit using light bulbs.

You could test this by unscrewing the middle bulb. The top and bottom bulbs will remain as bright as when all three bulbs were on.

If you unscrewed the bottom bulb, the top bulb would continue to shine without any change in its brightness.

Uses for parallel circuits

The electricity supply in your home, school and in most buildings is an example of parallel wiring. This means that you can connect as many items as you need to the electricity supply.

However, the more items you connect, the more power is needed to run them and, if you use a battery, the faster it will run out!

Summary
• A parallel circuit is made up of several loops, each connected directly to the power supply.
• No matter how many bulbs you connect to this circuit, they will all stay equally bright.

13

What circuits can do

Electricity can do much more than just make bulbs light. It can work other components, make heat and magnetism and even cause liquids to change.

Electricity can be used to make many things happen, not just light bulbs or work motors.

Many things at once

Circuits can be made to do many things at the same time. In Picture 1 you can see a circuit that shows some of these things. When the switch is closed, the buzzer will sound (electricity can produce sound); the motor will turn (electricity can cause movement); the bulb will light (electricity can produce light and heat); the compass will turn (electricity can make a coil of wire act as a magnet); the salty water will begin to bubble (electricity flows through liquids, and if you leave it connected long enough it can transfer metals in the liquid from one place to another); and the coil will pick up paper clips (another way that electricity can make magnetism).

Always make a loop

This is a parallel circuit, so all of these effects can go on at the same time. Notice that each component is in a loop with the battery, although some parts of the loop use shared wires.

▶ **(Picture 1) Heat, light, sound, movement and magnetism can be created using a circuit.**

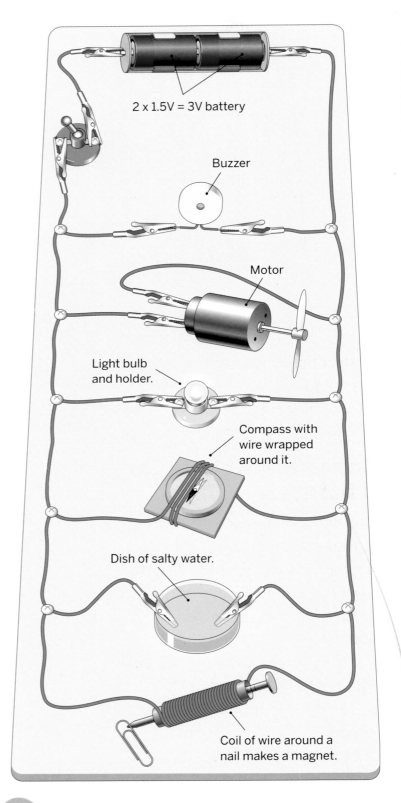

2 x 1.5V = 3V battery

Buzzer

Motor

Light bulb and holder.

Compass with wire wrapped around it.

Dish of salty water.

Coil of wire around a nail makes a magnet.

Weblink: www.CurriculumVisions.com

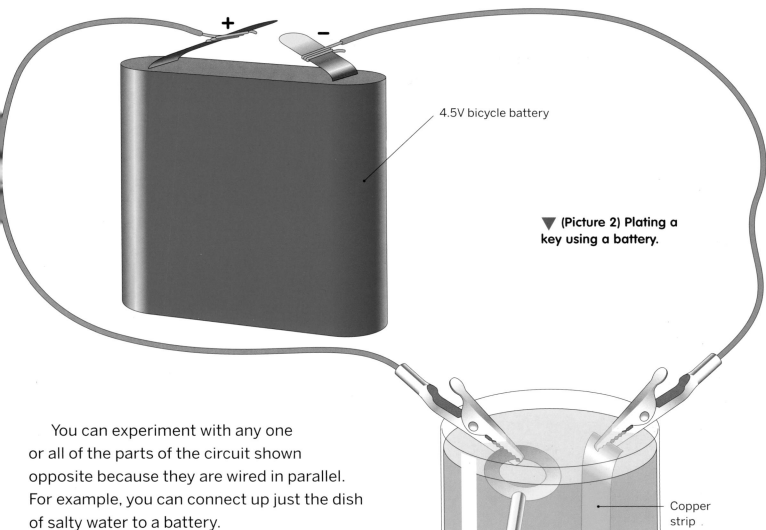

4.5V bicycle battery

▼ (Picture 2) Plating a key using a battery.

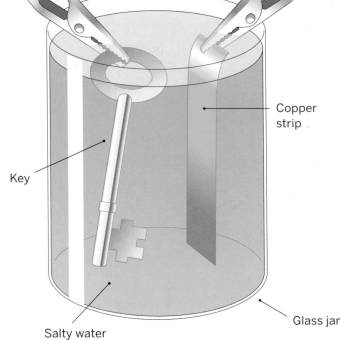

Copper strip

Key

Glass jar

Salty water

You can experiment with any one or all of the parts of the circuit shown opposite because they are wired in parallel. For example, you can connect up just the dish of salty water to a battery.

Coat a key with copper using a battery!

One of the things electricity can be used for is to move metals in a liquid from one object to another. This is called electroplating. You can use electroplating to cover a key with copper. To do this, you need to use a strip of copper and a key.

Connect up the battery as shown in Picture 2 and watch as the bright chromium is covered by a coat of orange-coloured copper. This is electroplating. You will not be able to scrape off the copper!

Summary

• Electricity can produce sound, it can cause movement, it can produce light and heat, it can turn a wire into a magnet and it can transfer metals from one place to another.

Weblink: www.CurriculumVisions.com

Fuses

A fuse is an emergency switch. It is a thin wire which will easily melt and break the flow of electricity when a circuit becomes overloaded.

Imagine a circuit wire as a pipe full of water. The wider the pipe, the more water it can carry. Normally, electrical currents flow quite slowly through the wires of a circuit, just as water might flow slowly through a pipe.

What happens when you try to force a lot of electricity around a circuit? The answer is that the electrical flow speeds up. Just as fast-moving water brushes against the walls of the pipe and warms it up, so fast-moving electricity makes a wire get warm.

Fuses

It is often dangerous to allow wires to heat up because they can produce fires. This is why we use a safety device called a **FUSE** (Picture 1).

A fuse is a small length of thin wire made of a metal that melts as it warms up (Picture 2). As soon as the wire melts, the circuit is broken. When this happens, people say that the 'fuse has blown'.

Fuse wire is kept in special safety tubes to prevent the melting wire from touching anything that could catch fire.

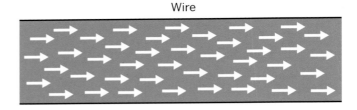

Wire

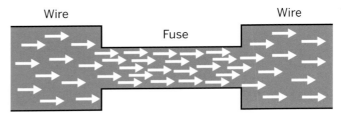

Wire · Fuse · Wire

▲ **(Picture 1) A fuse is a very thin wire with a low melting point. The voltage which the fuse can take is matched to the voltage of the circuit to make sure it is the first thing to fail.**

▼ **(Picture 2) The stages of a fuse blowing.**

No overload. Fuse wire is cool.

Overload beginning. Fuse wire heats up and expands.

Fuse wire melts safely inside tube and circuit is broken.

Weblink: www.CurriculumVisions.com

Fuses and circuits

Fuse wires have to be used carefully. If you have a thick fuse wire in a circuit where the other wires are thin, the fuse wire may not be the first to heat up and the whole purpose of the fuse would be lost. But if the fuse wire is too thin, it will keep melting and the circuit will never work. Fuses must be matched to the circuits they are used in.

The electrical equipment we use at home or at school – such as a kettle or toaster – each has its own fuse. The fuse is often in the plug. Picture 3 shows how fuses are used to protect sensitive equipment.

Fuses that are fitted inside plugs are always labelled to show what their values are. Lights, radios, TVs and the like are protected by either a 3A or a 5A fuse, while kettles and similar appliances are protected by a 13A fuse. A 13A fuse must *never* be used in a circuit for low-power electrical equipment.

Summary
- A fuse is used to protect circuit wires from overheating.
- A fuse is used to protect sensitive equipment such as computers.
- **The correct fuse must always be used.**

▲ (Picture 3) A computer is always fused. There will be a fuse in the computer case (and in the monitor case) and often in the mains plug, too.

Weblink: www.CurriculumVisions.com

Using electricity for heat

When a large current flows through a thin wire, it will get hot. This is how a heating element works.

Electricity is useful in many ways around the home. For example, when electricity flows through a wire, the flow of electricity causes the wire to heat up. Many pieces of electrical equipment contain wires that heat up in a controlled way.

 (Note: Of course, uncontrolled heating of wires is very dangerous.)

Heating elements

If you look at an electric fire (Picture 1) you will see that the heating part – called the heating element – is made of a coil of wire. This is a special type of wire that does not melt when it becomes red hot.

When the heater is switched on the current flows through the heating element just as it would flow through a bulb.

Remember that when a wire carries a large amount of electricity compared with its width, it can give out both heat and light. In some fires the light is used to give a 'warm' glow and, as a safety measure, to tell you that the heater is on.

Heat from electricity

Heating elements look very different, depending on where they are needed, but the principle is always the same.

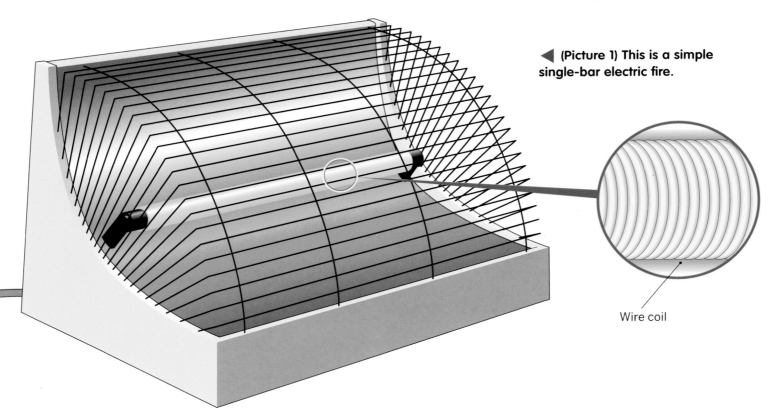

◀ **(Picture 1) This is a simple single-bar electric fire.**

Wire coil

Weblink: www.CurriculumVisions.com

▲ **(Picture 2) This shows the heating element in a toaster. The element is kept away from the bread by a wire cage inside the toaster.**

Here are common places where heating elements are found:

- ▶ Toasters (Picture 2).
- ▶ Electric kettles.
- ▶ Electric blankets.
- ▶ Electric heaters or fires (Picture 1).
- ▶ Electric water heaters (Picture 3).
- ▶ Electric showers.
- ▶ Electric hair dryers (Picture 4).
- ▶ Electric irons.
- ▶ Electric ovens, grills and hot plates.

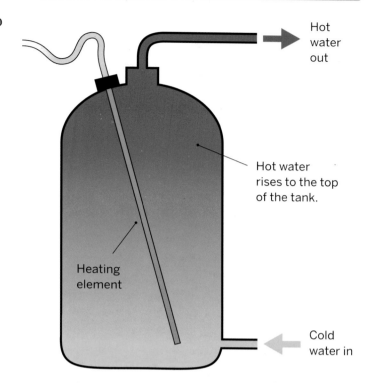

▲ **(Picture 3) This shows the heating element in an immersion heater inside a hot water cylinder. This is the kind of thing that provides hot water for your taps. The element has to be insulated from the water, so it is placed in a sealed tube with a thermostat in the top.**

▶ **(Picture 4) A hair dryer is like an electric fire, with the element exposed to the air. An electric fan is placed behind the element and it blows air through the element. The air warms up as it passes the element and emerges from the dryer.**

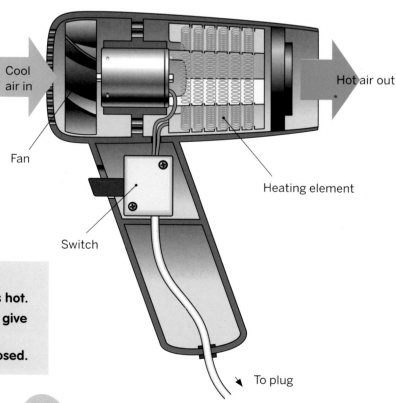

Summary
- When a large current flows through a wire it gets hot.
- When used in heating, wires are designed not to give out much light, as this is not wanted.
- All heating elements need to be kept safely enclosed.

Weblink: www.CurriculumVisions.com

Home circuits

Your home electricity supply makes use of the circuits and fuses shown on the previous pages.

The electricity running through the wires in your house uses all of the ideas you have seen in the earlier parts of this book. In particular you need to remember about parallel circuits (page 12) and fuses (page 16). In Pictures 1 and 2 you see all of these ideas put to good, safe use.

Supply

The electricity supply company connects your home to the cable in the street through a fuse box (**A**). This is to prevent an electrical problem in your home from causing problems to other homes nearby, or vice versa.

Meter

The meter (**B**) records the amount of electrical energy you use in your home every second. You can see how much you are using by watching the numbers change on the meter.

Wiring

Two wires go to every item that needs electricity (**C**). All of the portable items, such as TVs and irons, have plugs that push into wall sockets. In Picture 2 the **LIVE WIRE** (shown brown) brings electricity to the appliances, the **NEUTRAL WIRE** (shown blue) carries it away. The wire shown in green is also used in some circuits and is an **EARTH WIRE** (**D**). This is a protection device to carry electricity safely away if a fault develops.

The circuit for the sockets and the circuit for the lights are both examples of parallel circuits.

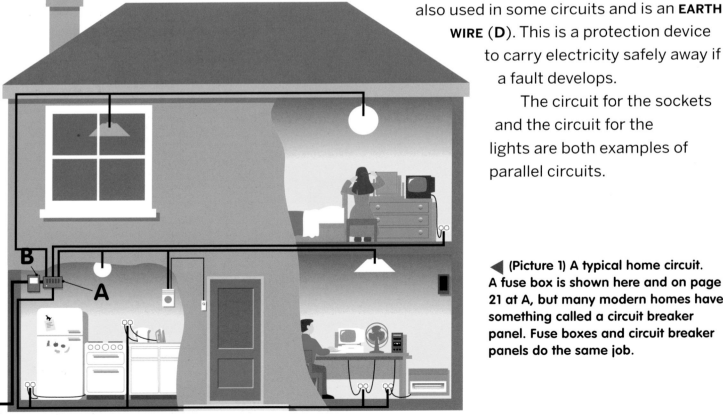

◄ (Picture 1) A typical home circuit. A fuse box is shown here and on page 21 at A, but many modern homes have something called a circuit breaker panel. Fuse boxes and circuit breaker panels do the same job.

Weblink: www.CurriculumVisions.com

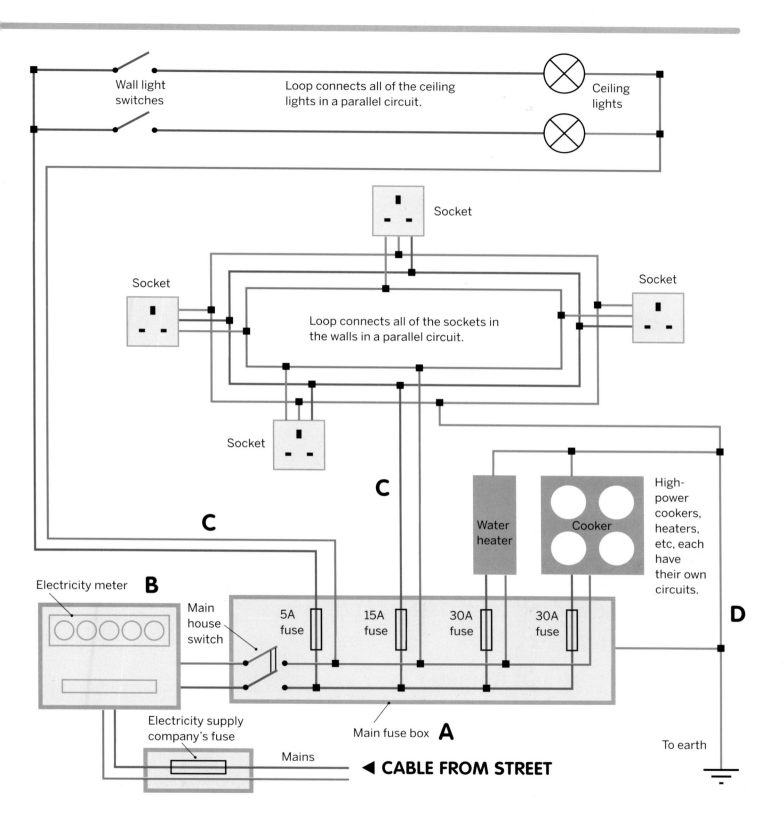

Wall light switches

Loop connects all of the ceiling lights in a parallel circuit.

Ceiling lights

Socket

Loop connects all of the sockets in the walls in a parallel circuit.

Socket

Socket

Socket

C

C

B

Electricity meter

Main house switch

5A fuse

15A fuse

30A fuse

30A fuse

Water heater

Cooker

High-power cookers, heaters, etc, each have their own circuits.

D

Electricity supply company's fuse

Mains

Main fuse box **A**

To earth

◀ **CABLE FROM STREET**

▲ (Picture 2) This wiring diagram shows the parallel circuits used to feed electricity through a home.

KEY

Live ————
Neutral ————
Earth ————

Summary
• The wiring in your home works on the principle of parallel loops.
• Each type of loop is protected by a fuse.

Power supplies

Most of the things we do in the modern world depend on a power supply. This is how electricity gets from a power station to homes and other buildings.

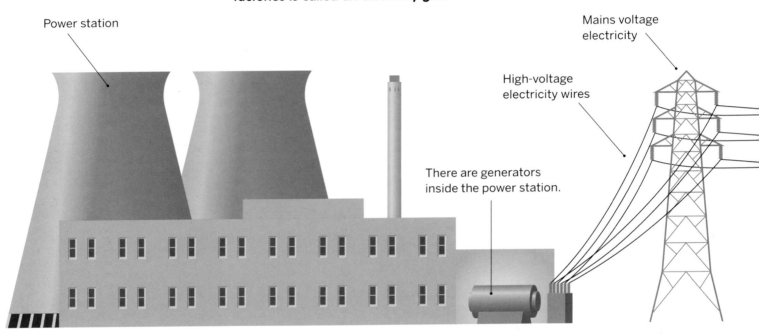

▼ (Picture 1) The way electricity is carried from power stations to homes, offices and factories is called an electricity grid.

Power station

Mains voltage electricity

High-voltage electricity wires

There are generators inside the power station.

MAINS ELECTRICITY is made, or generated, in a power station (Picture 1).

Getting power to our homes

Once the electricity has been generated, it must be moved to where it is needed. The wires from the power station carry a very high voltage so they must be kept safely away from people. This can be done by putting them in plastic sleeves and burying them in the ground (Picture 3), or by hanging them in the air (Picture 2). It is very expensive to bury cables, so outside cities most cables are hung in the air from towers, or pylons. Air is used as a cheap insulator (Picture 2).

Picture 1 shows how power is taken from a power station to factories, offices and homes. The pattern of cables is called an **ELECTRICITY GRID**. The voltage in the cables from a power station is often as much as 400,000 volts. This is the best voltage to carry electricity long distances.

When the electricity supply gets near to the place where it is needed, the voltage is stepped down to about 240V.

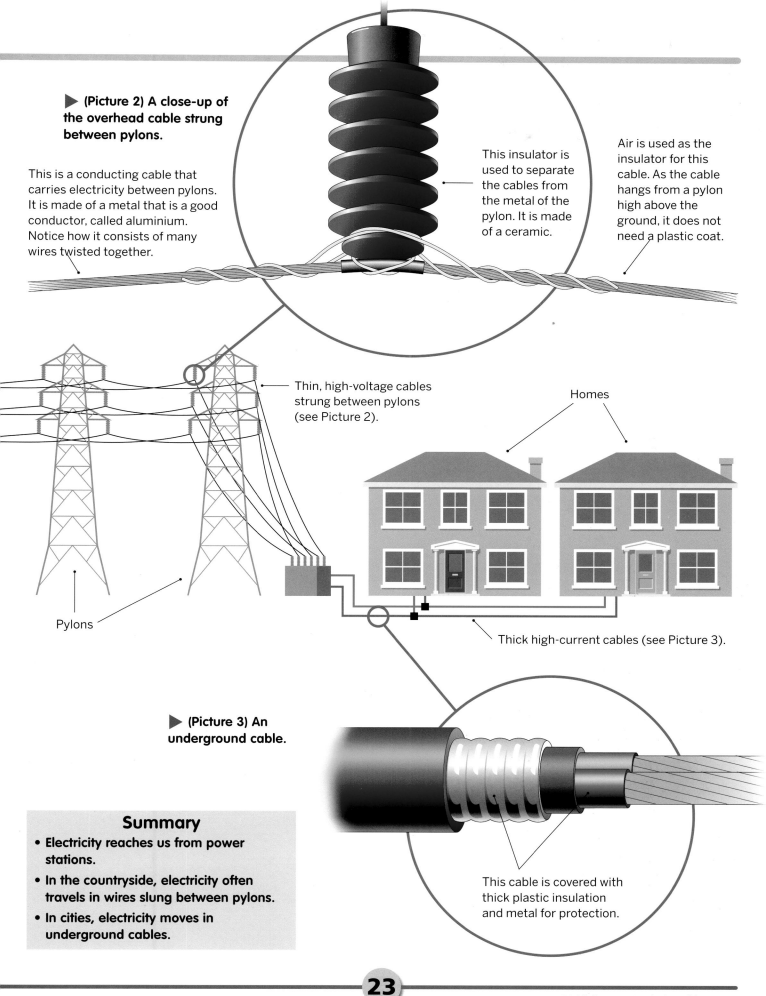

▶ **(Picture 2) A close-up of the overhead cable strung between pylons.**

This is a conducting cable that carries electricity between pylons. It is made of a metal that is a good conductor, called aluminium. Notice how it consists of many wires twisted together.

This insulator is used to separate the cables from the metal of the pylon. It is made of a ceramic.

Air is used as the insulator for this cable. As the cable hangs from a pylon high above the ground, it does not need a plastic coat.

Thin, high-voltage cables strung between pylons (see Picture 2).

Homes

Pylons

Thick high-current cables (see Picture 3).

▶ **(Picture 3) An underground cable.**

This cable is covered with thick plastic insulation and metal for protection.

Summary
- Electricity reaches us from power stations.
- In the countryside, electricity often travels in wires slung between pylons.
- In cities, electricity moves in underground cables.

23

Index

Curriculum Visions

Science@School

Teacher's Guide

There is a Teacher's Guide to accompany this book, available only from the publisher.

There's much more online including videos

You will find multimedia resources covering this and ALL 37 QCA Key Stage 1 and 2 science units as well as history, geography, religion, MFL, maths, music, spelling and more at:

www.CurriculumVisions.com

(Subscription required)

A CVP Book
This second edition © Atlantic Europe Publishing 2012

First edition 2002. First reprint 2005. Second reprint 2007.

Author
Brian Knapp, BSc, PhD

Educational Consultant
Peter Riley, BSc, C Biol, MI Biol, PGCE

Senior Designer
Adele Humphries, BA, PGCE

Editor
Lisa Magloff, MA

Illustrations
David Woodroffe

Designed and produced by
Atlantic Europe Publishing

Printed in China by
WKT Company Ltd

Volume 6G Changing circuits 2nd Edition – Curriculum Visions Science@School
A CIP record for this book is available from the British Library.

Paperback ISBN 978 1 86214 706 5

Picture credits
All photographs are from the Earthscape Picture Library.